Cool Stuff About Planets!

Lisa James

Contents

- So, Did You Know ...? 2
- Mercury 6
- Venus 8
- Earth 10
- Mars 12
- Jupiter 14
- Saturn 16
- Uranus 18
- Neptune 20
- Pluto 22
- Learn More 23
- Glossary and Index 24

So, Did You Know ...?

- Did you know that Neptune was only **discovered** 150 years ago?
- Did you know that an 11-year-old girl named Pluto?

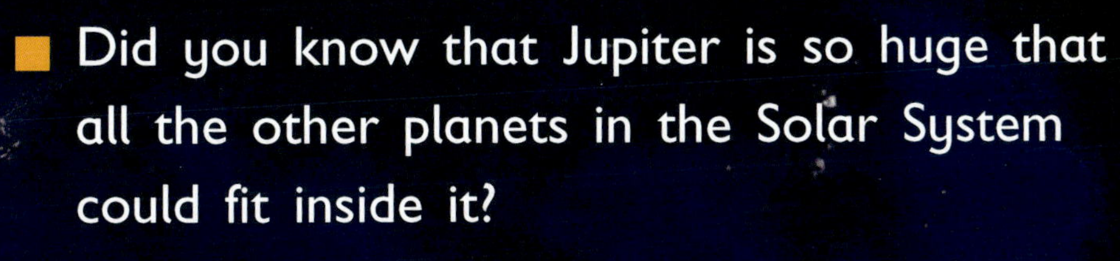

- Did you know that Jupiter is so huge that all the other planets in the Solar System could fit inside it?
- If you turn the page you will learn some more really cool stuff about planets!

The Solar System

- The Solar System is the Sun and the planets that move around it.

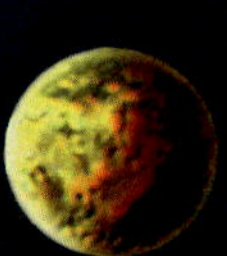

Jupiter Saturn Uranus Neptune

Mercury

- Did you know that Mercury is the smallest planet in our Solar System?
- It is also the fastest planet to **orbit** the Sun. It takes 88 Earth days for Mercury to move around the Sun.
- One day on Mercury is as long as 59 Earth days!

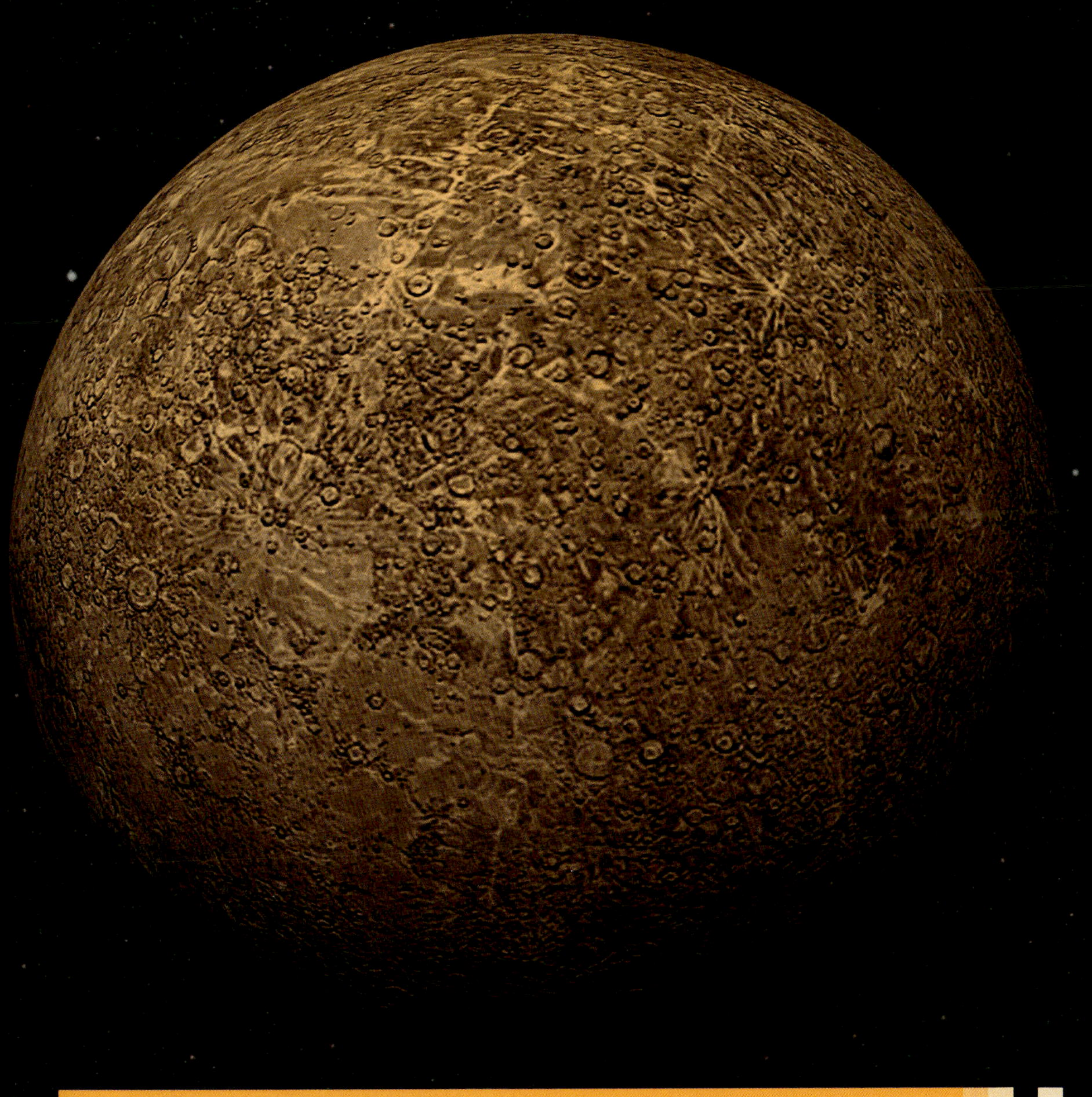

Distance from Sun	46 million km
Time taken to orbit the Sun	88 Earth days
Time taken to spin	59 Earth days
Number of moons	0

Venus

- Did you know that, from Earth, Venus looks brighter than any star in the sky? But Venus has lots of clouds around it.

Most of Venus is covered by **lava flows** from **volcanoes**.

Distance from Sun	108 million km
Time taken to orbit the Sun	225 Earth days
Time taken to spin	243 Earth days
Number of moons	0

- Did you know that the first person to see Earth from space was the astronaut Yuri Gagarin? That was in 1961.

Yuri Gagarin

- From space, Earth looks blue. This is because most of Earth is covered in water.
- Earth is the largest of the **rocky planets**. It is the only planet known to have life.

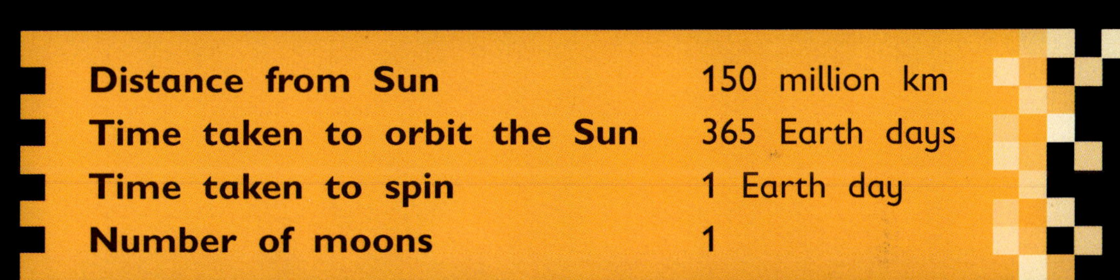

Distance from Sun	150 million km
Time taken to orbit the Sun	365 Earth days
Time taken to spin	1 Earth day
Number of moons	1

Mars

- Did you know that Mars has the largest volcano in the Solar System?

Mars also has the longest **canyon** in the Solar System. It would reach across Australia.

Distance from Sun	229 million km
Time taken to orbit the Sun	687 Earth days
Time taken to spin	1 Earth day
Number of moons	2

Jupiter

21

- Did you know that Jupiter is the biggest planet in the Solar System? It is so big that its **gravity** can suck in its moons.
- Jupiter's Great Red Spot is the biggest, most **violent** storm in the Solar System. It is three times the size of Earth!

Distance from Sun	778 million km
Time taken to orbit the Sun	12 Earth years
Time taken to spin	10 Earth hours
Number of moons	over 60

Great Red Spot

- Did you know that Saturn is the second biggest planet in the Solar System? But it is so light that it could float on water.

- Saturn has beautiful rings around it. Scientists think these rings are made of bits of dust and ice.

Distance from Sun	1429 million km
Time taken to orbit the Sun	29 Earth years
Time taken to spin	10 Earth hours
Number of moons	61

Uranus

- Did you know that Uranus is tipped on its side? It does not spin around like other planets. It rolls like a ball around the Sun.
- Uranus takes 84 years to orbit the Sun. So, each side of Uranus gets 42 years of day and then 42 years of night.

Distance from Sun	2871 million km
Time taken to orbit the Sun	84 Earth years
Time taken to spin	17 Earth hours
Number of moons	27

Neptune

- Neptune is a windy planet! It has the strongest winds of any planet in the Solar System.

Did you know that Neptune's biggest moon, Triton, is moving closer to Neptune?

Distance from Sun	4504 million km
Time taken to orbit the Sun	165 Earth years
Time taken to spin	16 Earth hours
Number of moons	13

Pluto

P

- Did you know that Pluto used to be a planet, but now it is **not** a planet? It is a **dwarf planet**.
- Scientists thought Pluto was too small to be a planet. Pluto also does not have an orbit like the other planets.
- There are lots of dwarf planets in the Solar System and more are being found all the time.

Learn More

- As scientists learn more, the things we know about planets change.
- Look up into the night sky. There are always more cool facts to learn about planets!

Glossary

- **canyon** — a long, deep valley with steep sides
- **discovered** — found out something for the first time
- **dwarf planet** — an object that travels around the Sun. But it is not a moon.
- **gravity** — a force which tries to pull objects towards each other
- **lava flows** — melted rock that flows above ground
- **orbit** — the path one object takes around another object
- **rocky planets** — planets mostly made up of rock. Mercury, Venus, Earth and Mars are rocky planets.
- **violent** — using extreme force
- **volcanoes** — openings in a planet's crust that push molten rock to the surface